1

Since I was very young, I knew I was Aboriginal. My mother is Aboriginal but my father is not. I am Aboriginal because my mother is Aboriginal. Her ancestors are from the Wiradjuri Nation. As a child I had a strong connection to the land and animals. I felt more comfortable to be out in nature than inside the house. I often looked very closely at the trees, and birds, and sky, and stars. I believed that there was a mighty creator who made all things.

3

My brothers are also Aboriginal.
We would play lots as children.
We would climb and run and
swim. We would walk through
the bush and see lizards and
snakes. I wasn't scared of
snakes because I saw them
often. We would camp in the
dunes near the beach and make
a campfire. We would wake
early and go swimming.

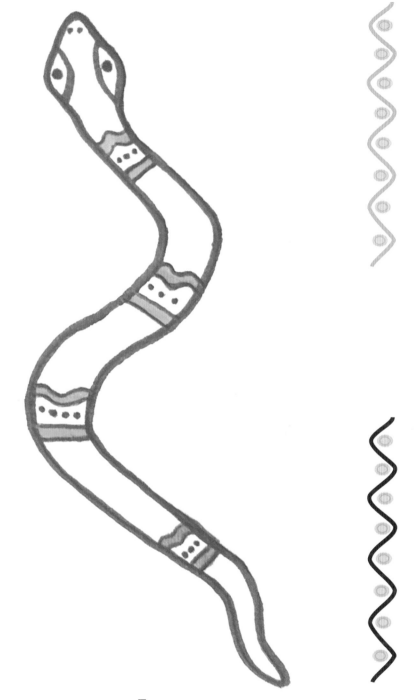

5

Some of my friends were also Aboriginal. Some had light skin and some had dark skin but we were still Aboriginal. Aboriginal people have lots of different skin tones. What makes them Aboriginal is not only their skin colour. It is that their ancestors were Aboriginal. It is also because they like to be Aboriginal and live the culture. For different reasons some Aboriginal people haven't learnt about their culture. There are people who can teach them if they want to learn.

My older Aboriginal friends taught me to hunt and gather. They taught me how to spear fish and catch crabs in traps and collect pipis with my feet. They taught me what plants to eat and not eat. We ate pigface plants on the dunes after a long swim. We ate lilly pilly fruit in the bush after a long walk. If we caught fish, we would share them with each other. We would give some to other families. That way, everyone had something to eat.

I learned to dance from my Aboriginal Uncles. They were not my blood uncles but because they are respected men, I call them Uncles. They would come to my school and show me how to dance. The boys would learn from the Uncles and the girls would learn from the Aunties. They showed me how to dance like the kangaroo, emu, snake, and sea eagle. They taught me how to do shake a leg and strike a pose. They told me I am 'deadly'. This means really good!

11

Each year, all the Aboriginal students at my school would go away on a camp where we learned more about our culture. Some of the Uncles and Aunties came and taught us. We went to Stradbroke Island near Brisbane. We went on a ferry and camped near the beach. The Aboriginal people of Stradbroke were friendly and taught us about their land and animals. Together we explored the land and the waterholes and looked at goannas.

13

I liked surfing each day. I was part of a surfboard riders group with lots of Aboriginal surfers. We surfed at Fingal Head in Northern New South Wales. Fingal Head is a very special place with a large Aboriginal community. They do many good things for the community. The surfers from Fingal showed me how to surf better. They did Aboriginal dancing and cooking too.

15

When I finished school, I moved away from my hometown and went to university. At university there was an Aboriginal student centre. This was a place where Aboriginal students could meet each other and the support staff.

We helped each other with our studies. We helped each other if we missed home. The Elders from the community came and welcomed us to their land. They gave us their blessing and best wishes for our studies. The Elders were very kind.

17

When I was at university, I learned how to do Aboriginal art. I made lots of drawings and paintings. I made clap sticks and spears. I learned to make music and rap about my Aboriginal culture. Sometimes we had big events and many Aboriginal people would come from other areas. Many non-Aboriginal people would come and watch the culture and buy some art. I would do my rap music in front of the crowd.

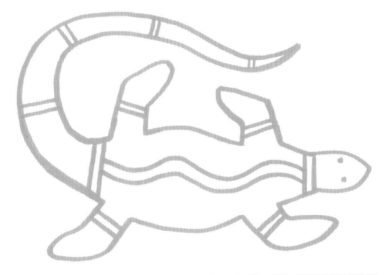

19

One day, I met a kind Aboriginal Elder. I called her Aunty to show her respect. She is a Christian minister and she invited me to her Aboriginal Church. I met many Aboriginal Christians and I learned about the love of Jesus. The people there were loving too. They also taught me about their language. They called God 'Marmung'. They called children 'Jarjums'. They call themselves 'Goori' which means Aboriginal people.

21

I have two sons. They are two and four. They are Aboriginal because I am Aboriginal and I am their Dad. I teach them how to dance and play the didgeridoo. I teach them how to climb and jump and swim. I teach them to respect people and I teach them language. I also teach them about the love of Jesus. My children are now learning about their culture. When they are older they will teach their children about Aboriginal culture. This is how Aboriginal people keep our culture alive.

Word bank

Aboriginal

ancestors

Wiradjuri

connection

comfortable

pipis

lilly pilly

respected

kangaroo

emu

deadly

assembly

Brisbane

Fingal Head

special

community

university

Christian

minister

Marmung

Jarjums

Goori